Money Spells

Money
Spells

Josephine Collins

RYLAND
PETERS
& SMALL

LONDON NEW YORK

Designer *Sarah Walden*
Senior Editor *Clare Double*
Picture Research *Claire Hector*
Production *Deborah Wehner*
Art Director *Gabriella Le Grazie*
Publishing Director *Alison Starling*

Editorial Consultant *Christina Rodenbeck*

First published in the United States
in 2004 by Ryland Peters & Small, Inc.
519 Broadway, 5th Floor
New York NY 10012

www.rylandpeters.com

ISBN 1 84172 620 6

Printed and bound in China

contents

How to use this book   6

Tools for Abundance   7

Being a Money Magnet   12

Money Moon Magic   22

Boosting Business   32

Overcoming Obstacles   42

Lottery Luck   50

Staying in the Flow   58

Picture credits   64

How to use this book

For the modern witch, money is a form of energy, which can be directed and increased. Think of credit as a boost of positive energy, and debt (even an overdraft) as a lack of energy, and you'll find it easier to manipulate the cash flow in your life.

Wealth means different things to different people, so before you undertake any of the spells in this book, think about what wealth means to you. Why do you want to be more prosperous, and how much money would you need in order to feel truly wealthy? Once you start to think about it, you may find that it's not so much quantity that's important, but the feeling of having enough for your desires and needs.

Money Spells *contains a host of ideas for increasing the flow of abundance into your life, so use these alongside the spells. Before you start, read through "Tools for Abundance" (pages 7–11), then take a look through the book and see which spell best suits your needs. Always remember that what goes out into the universe will come back to you, so respect the power of your spell work and keep it positive.*

Tools for Abundance

Your magical toolkit

The tools you use in magic are there to symbolize
your intentions and connect you to the power of the
universe. Candles, salt, incense, and water are often
used to represent the four elements, which can be
called on to empower your spell. Colors, symbols,
crystals, oils, and herbs are just some of the other
tools that can represent your desires. By using them
with your focused attention, emotional desire, vision,
and words, you can connect to your goal.

Tools for money and attracting wealth

Colors: *Gold, green, silver (wealth); purple (success), red (action).*

Crystals: *Amethyst (creative thinking), aventurine, citrine, jade (financial success), lodestone (attraction), obsidian (financial security), onyx, tiger-eye (confidence).*

Runes: *Beorc (beginnings and growth), Feoh (wealth and possessions), Ger (fruition of efforts).*

Tarot cards: *The Emperor (wealth), the Empress (fruitfulness), the Star (fulfillment), the Sun (success), the Ten of Coins (riches).*

Planetary symbols: *Jupiter (luck and growth), the Sun (success).*

Herbs and oils: *Almond, basil, bergamot (money, success), cinnamon, cloves, frankincense (material attraction), honeysuckle (money), juniper (protection), marigolds (wealth, fame), nutmeg (prosperity), pine, rosemary (clarity of purpose, money), sandalwood (purification).*

Numbers: *1 = leadership, 3 = growth, 5 = freedom, 8 = material stability, 9 = ambition, 10 = success.*

Clearing your energy field

Before you start spell working, it's important to
clear your energy field and dispel any negativity
that might get in the way of your success. The
meditation opposite will help to clear your energy
and put you in a more positive frame of mind.

Clearing your energy meditation

Find a quiet time and a place where you won't be disturbed. Close your eyes. Sit with a straight back. Take a breath. As you breathe out, release any tension you feel, then breathe in a feeling of relaxation.

Imagine an orange light flowing down through the top of your head, cascading into and around your body.

See this orange light collecting any negative thoughts, emotions, or physical feelings that you are holding in and around your body.

Now see the orange light moving down through your body, taking any negativity with it, and then moving out through the soles of your feet into the earth.

Once you have done this, visualize pure white energy coming down through the top of your head, rejuvenating and healing you, and bringing with it a feeling of optimism and positivity.

Then thank the universe for cleansing your energy field, and open your eyes, feeling your presence back in your body.

Being a Money Magnet

Some people are naturally better at attracting money than others, but if you want to increase your chances of success with your spell work, follow the ten steps below.

Ten steps to successful spell working

1 Know what you want to attract. Be clear about how much money you want to draw into your life.

2 Be willing to take the practical action needed. Without physical action, your spell will not be complete.

3 Believe you can have it. Think of all the reasons why you should receive this prosperity.

4 Use your imagination. See yourself having achieved your goal.

5 Use the power of words. Speak to yourself positively about your ability to reach your goals.

6 *Release your desire to the universe. Let your request go out into the universe to hook up with what you want.*

7 *Listen to your intuitive urges. These often come in the form of inspiration or a strong desire to do something.*

8 *Know why you want it. Write down the reasons that you want to attract a particular amount of money.*

9 *Be open to receive. Expect your goal to materialize.*

10 *Thank the universe. Have an attitude of gratitude.*

Be a money magnet

This spell will make your energy more magnetic to money.

You will need:
a white candle
pen and paper

Sit with a straight back. Light your candle and place it in front of you. Write down the sum of money you would like to attract. It should be an amount you can easily imagine receiving. Look into the candle flame and ask the power of the universe to assist you in your goal.

Now imagine a powerful white light building around your solar plexus (i.e. the pit of your stomach). See a branch from this light going out to connect you to the amount you want.

Visualize the money coming to you. Keep on generating energy until you feel it has connected with your desire.

Then draw the branch of light back into your solar plexus. Tell yourself that you are open to receive this amount of money, thank the universe, and put out your candle.

After you've finished the spell, let it go out of your mind and turn your attention to something else. You can do this spell every week until you see results.

The magic talisman

A talisman works by attracting your desire to you.

Light your candle and incense, and place them in front of you, along with your glass of water and talisman.

You will need:
a white candle
sandalwood incense
a glass of water
a symbolic talisman
(this could be a coin,
pendant, or crystal)
sea salt or kosher salt
(use ordinary salt if
these are not available)

Concentrate for a moment on what you would like your talisman to attract. Then sprinkle a few pinches of salt into the glass of water and say:
With this salt, I consecrate this water, may whatever it touches be blessed with white light.

Sprinkle a drop of water onto your talisman and say:
With this sacred water, I consecrate this talisman to help me … (state your intention).

Then pass the talisman through the flame of the candle and say:
With this flame, I cleanse this talisman to help me … (state your intention).

Pass the talisman through the smoke from the incense and say:
With this incense, I imprint this talisman to help me ... (state your intention).

See yourself holding your talisman after achieving your desire. Thank the universe, extinguish the candle and incense, and come back to your physical awareness.

Wealth wand spell

This is a great spell if you want to increase the money you have already saved. You can also use your wand in other spells for extra luck.

You will need:
a willow branch
sandpaper
almond oil
a small amethyst crystal
copper wire
gold, silver, or green ribbon

First make your wand. Choose a branch from a willow tree. Thank the tree for allowing you to cut it. Remove the bark and sand it down, then rub in some almond oil.

At the end of the branch that was not attached to the tree, attach your amethyst crystal using the copper wire. Now inscribe your wand with any symbols that feel relevant to you, for example, the sign of Jupiter ($2\!\!\!/$) or a dollar sign. Then tie gold, silver, or green ribbon around your wand.

Perform this spell on a Friday at the time of a New or Waxing Moon.

Hold the wand in the hand that you write with, and imagine it being charged with gold light. Say, as you point to the relevant directions:

To my right,
To my left,
Above me and below:
Come on magic wand,
Make my money grow!

Money Moon Magic

Working with the Moon

Not only does the Moon control the ebb and
flow of the tide, but it is also believed to have
a powerful influence over all living things. By
carrying out a spell at the right time, you can use
the Moon's natural energy to boost its outcome.

The Moon's phases

Each Moon cycle lasts about thirty days and begins with a New
Moon, which is when the Moon is virtually invisible. From this
phase, the Moon gradually increases in size until it becomes
a Full Moon. Until this point, the Moon is waxing (getting
bigger). After a Full Moon, the Moon wanes (gets smaller)
until it finally disappears and turns into a New Moon once
again. Many ordinary diaries mark the phases of the Moon.

Using the Moon's phases for spell work

The New Moon: *Choose spells that focus on new beginnings.*

The Waxing Moon: *Choose spells that work on increasing something in your life.*

The Full Moon: *Choose spells that work on bringing a resolution to a project or problem.*

The Waning Moon: *Choose spells that deal with reducing problems or obstacles.*

You will need:
a New Moon
a large white candle
a compass
four green candles
a new silver dollar
or dollar bill

New Moon new wealth

Use this New Moon spell to generate a new source of wealth and success.

Take the white candle and, using the compass, place the four green candles around it to form a square, so they point to the four directions North, South, East, and West.

Place the dollar in front of the white candle and say:
At this New Moon, with this new coin/bill, I plant the seeds of my desire.
That I may attract great wealth and success, to this I do aspire.
I light each candle one by one to make my vision real,
And with my focused energy to the New Moon I appeal.

Light the white candle and say:
Help me, New Moon, to keep my desire burning.

Then as you light the relevant green candles say:
Money flow from the North,
Money flow from the South,
Money flow from the East,
Money flow from the West.

Focus on the flames. See yourself
achieving your vision and say:
So may it be.

Then extinguish the candles
and expect to see new
wealth flourishing.

Waxing wealth Moon

This is a versatile spell to make your money grow. It's good for boosting an investment or to encourage more cash to come your way.

Light the purple candle and place it in front of you with your symbol. On the piece of paper, write what you want to achieve. Then take a pinch of each herb and sprinkle it over the paper, saying three times:
Herbs of purpose, herbs of the earth, bless my desire and make it work.

Then look into the candle flame and visualize achieving your desire. Say:
By the power of the Waxing Moon my money/ investment/savings now expands,
Lady Luck with her guiding light now lends her helping hands.
By the power of the Waxing Moon these seeds of success I sow,
Lady Luck with her power to magnify, helps my money/ investment/savings grow.

You will need:
a Waxing Moon
a purple candle
a symbol of what you want to increase, such as a share certificate, savings book, or wallet
pen and paper
a few pinches of dried basil and rosemary

Finally, extinguish the candle and bury the paper and herbs somewhere nice outside, in your garden if you have one.

Full Moon full purse

Improve your intuitive money-making skills.

In the light of a Full Moon, place your silver coin in your open
palm and say:
*Dear Goddess Moon, shine down your rays upon my
open palm,
And with your powers to increase, create for me a charm.*

You will need:
*a Full Moon
a silver coin
a coin purse
or wallet*

Place the coin in your coin purse or wallet and say:
*As I place this coin inside my purse to magnetize my vision,
I make myself receptive to your help with each decision.
Dear Goddess Moon, I take the steps to keep my money
growing,
And thank you for your wisdom and your help to keep my
money flowing.*

After this, be ready to act on your intuitive urgings to increase
your wealth.

Waning Moon let go let flow

Use this spell to rid yourself of obstacles that have been holding back your flow of wealth.

Light the candle and look into the flame, saying:
Waning Moon, as you shrink in size,
Dissolve all obstacles and fear
So that when the Moon is born again,
My path to abundance is clear.

You will need:
a night of the
Waning Moon (this
could be a night or
two after a Full
Moon, and should be
at least four nights
before a New Moon)
a white candle

Visualize any obstacles dissolving as the candle burns down, and then see money coming to you with ease.

Boosting Business

Boosting your business luck

There are many magical tricks you can use to increase your business success. Below are some suggestions:

1 Keep your workplace organized to encourage money to flow your way.

2 Repeat a prosperity affirmation three times whenever you enter your office.

3 Have a focal point on your desk that reminds you of abundance.

4 Place eight pieces of jade on top of your computer to increase your earning potential.

5 Place a money tree on your desk, with three coins underneath it, to encourage financial growth.

6 *Place a black stone such as onyx, tourmaline, or obsidian in your work area to encourage financial security.*

7 *Stick the symbol of the planet Jupiter (♃) where you will see it often, to encourage luck, expansion, and growth.*

8 *Hang a gold star above your desk to encourage luck and success.*

9 *Place a figure of a lion or a dragon on your desk to enhance your power and attract wealth. Or place an elephant (he must have his trunk up and pointing towards the door) on your desk to increase your wealth.*

10 *Place a citrine crystal by your telephone, mailbox, or computer to help open up lines of communication.*

Successful enterprise

If you're launching a new business, this is the spell for you.

On a Thursday when the Moon is waxing, anoint the green candle with the oil and as you do, repeat three times: *God and Goddess, empower my prayer.*

Now place the candle in front of you with the coin in front of the candle, about an inch away.

You will need:
a Waxing Moon
a green candle
clove oil
a shiny coin
three green stones
(for example, jade,
malachite, or
aventurine)

Place the three stones around the candle, to the right, to the left, and in the center, between the candle and the coin. Say three times:
Let this enterprise be blessed, let my business help many,
Let my work be well received, let abundance come in plenty,
As the days turn into weeks, and the weeks turn into months,
Let this coin attract to me great wealth, as my loving work is done.

Now light the green candle and as you do, visualize all the good things this business enterprise will bring.

Extinguish the candle and carry the coin around with you to enhance your luck. Make sure you have it with you for business meetings.

Lucky loan

If you're looking for credit,
lucky Jupiter can help.

You will need:
sandalwood incense
your loan document or letter

On a Wednesday morning, light some sandalwood incense. Then pass your loan form, or letter requesting the loan, through the smoke and say:
Oh Jupiter, hear my plea, bless this loan form/letter and bring this loan to me.

Lick your finger and use it to draw the sign of Jupiter ($\mathcal{2}$) on the back of your form. Do this on the back of every page.

Then turn the pages face up again. Look at them and visualize a positive response.

On Thursday morning, place the proposal in an envelope. Before mailing it, lick the index finger of the hand you write with, and draw the sign of Jupiter on the envelope. As you do so, say the following:
Jupiter, great planet of expansion and luck, bring your charm to this proposal and make it a success.

Kiss the envelope and post it.

boosting business

Tarot spell for getting a pay increase

Use the magical symbolism of tarot cards to get a raise.

Take a piece of green paper and write down the name of the person who is in a position to give you the raise.

To represent this person, choose the Emperor card for a man, or the Empress for a woman. Place the card on the paper.

On the second piece of paper, write down the amount of money that you would like from your raise as an affirmation, as though you have already received it. For example, "I now receive a pay raise of $3,000."

Place the Sun, the Star, and the Ten of Coins cards on top of the affirmation paper.

You will need:
three pieces of
green paper
a pen
tarot cards: the
Emperor or Empress,
the Sun, the Star,
and the Ten of Coins
basil oil

Take the last piece of paper, and with your basil oil, write a large figure eight on it. Place this paper on top of the other two pieces of paper.

Then repeat your affirmation three times and visualize yourself receiving the news that you have been given the pay raise.

Overcoming Obstacles

A prosperous attitude

There are times in most people's lives when
money matters get a bit stressful. Maybe you find yourself in
a situation where you don't have enough money to cover your
basic costs, you may have lent money to someone but are finding
it hard to get it back, or perhaps things have moved onto a more
serious level and you've taken legal proceedings to recover your money.

If you find yourself in any of these tricky situations, the following spells
will help. There are also many magical things you can do to protect
yourself and turn your luck around, such as the following.

To bolster security and protection, place two lions or dragons either side of your gate or door.

To encourage your life to run smoothly, make sure everything in your house is repaired and working properly.

To get good fortune flowing, keep your garden free from weeds.

To gain a clear perspective, clean mirrors and windows regularly.

If you need to go to court, try to schedule your appearance for a Thursday, when luck will be on your side.

To protect your home, hang a sprig of juniper upside down from a red ribbon by your windows and doors.

To bring good luck into your home, place a sprig of basil, a magnet, and five new coins above your door.

To encourage prosperity, dab bergamot essential oil on your checkbook, bank statements, and wallet.

To boost your money luck, carry a shiny horse chestnut or an acorn in your pocket.

To add luck to a financial transaction, wash your hands in chamomile tea before doing the deal.

Legal luck

You will need:
a large white candle
two green candles
a purple candle

If you ever have to go to court to get your money back from someone, make sure you ask Archangel Michael to help you.

Place the white candle in front of you, the green candles to the left, and the purple candle to the right.

Visualize the outcome you would like to achieve, and as you do, imagine the presence of a powerful white angel who has come to you to assist you in your fight. Light the white candle, followed by the purple candle, and then the green ones, and say the following words:

Archangel Michael, come to me in love and truth and light
Bring back to me the money owed
And protect me in my fight.
Archangel Michael, be with me, empower me with your might
Let the scales of justice tip in favor of truth
And confirm that I am right.

Thank Archangel Michael for his help. Extinguish the two green candles, then the purple candle, and lastly the white candle.

Quick money creator

If you need a quick cash fix, use this spell.

Put the white candle in front of you on the left and the green candle on the right, with a nine-inch gap between them.

You will need:
a white candle
a green candle

Light the candles and say three times:
Money, my friend, come to me.
I need your help, come quickly.
Wealth in abundance, three times three,
Fulfill my needs and come to me.

Thank the universe, and let the candles burn for nine minutes. Repeat at 9 p.m. for nine consecutive nights, moving the green candle an inch closer to the white candle each day.

Getting back money you're owed

You will need:

a shiny silver coin

a well or large bowl of water

Use this spell to get money returned to you.

Do this outside. Stand by your well or bowl and say:
I gave (amount of money) in good faith,
And now (name of person) must repay.
The wheel of fortune now completes the circle;
From (name of person and amount of money) comes
my way.

Then throw your silver coin into the well or bowl of water, saying:
As I throw this coin into the well, all obstacles dissolve,
All money owed me is paid back and outstanding
debts resolved.
I call upon the water to charge my special spell,
And let the powers of magic begin here in this
wishing well.

Lottery Luck

Lucky numbers

Numbers have been used throughout history for
the purposes of self-discovery, prediction, and spell work.
Each number, particularly those between one and ten, has a
unique meaning, and in magic this meaning can be used to
draw to you something you want.

If you feel an affinity with numbers, you may want to add
them to your spell work. You can do this by inscribing a
particular number on your main spell candle, or you
can draw a number that relates to what you want
on a piece of paper and place it in front of
you when you do your spell.

Numbers and their mystical meanings

1 *Leadership, determination*
2 *Partnership, co-operation*
3 *Creativity, learning*
4 *Stability, dedication*
5 *Enterprise, freedom*
6 *Harmony, balance*
7 *Mysticism, psychic power,*
introspection
8 *Business sense, material power*
9 *Action, ambition*
10 *Fulfillment, success*

You can also represent numbers with playing cards. If you do, make sure you choose diamonds for a money spell, and clubs if it involves work. Ideas are represented by spades, and love by hearts.

Winners' luck

You will need:

a green candle for each of the numbers you choose

a gold candle if there is a bonus number

a lottery ticket

pen and paper

a pinch each of ground cloves, cinnamon, and nutmeg

Do this spell before you buy a lottery ticket, to discover your lucky numbers.

Place the green candles in a row in front of you, with the gold candle at the end on the right, and light them. Place the lottery ticket form in front of them.

Say to yourself:
Divine guidance, please give me the numbers to bring me prosperity.

Stare into the flame of the first candle, let a number come into your head, and write it down. Do the same with the remaining candles until you have all the numbers written down. Now sprinkle the lottery ticket form with cloves, cinnamon, and nutmeg, and extinguish the candles.

Before you hand in the form, brush off the spices and say to yourself:
I am open to receive this gift.

Gambler's abundance oil spell

You will need:
a New Moon
a magnet
half a cup of
vegetable oil
frankincense,
cinnamon, and
lemon essential oils
a pinch of nutmeg
playing cards—
ten, Jack, Queen,
King, and ace of
diamonds

Use the suit of diamonds to generate your own lucky streak.

On the day after a New Moon, place a magnet in half a cup of vegetable oil. Let it sit for three days and nights on a windowsill.

Then take the magnet out, and add to the vegetable oil two drops of frankincense oil, one drop of cinnamon oil, one drop of lemon oil, and a pinch of nutmeg. Stir well.

The night before you gamble, pick up the five cards in the hand you write with, one by one, and anoint the back of each with the oil, saying the relevant phrase as you place each card in front of you:

The Jack of diamonds connects me to winners' luck,
The Queen of diamonds to conquest,
The King of diamonds shows I'm the best,
And the ace of diamonds fulfills my success.

Then kiss the ten of diamonds and say,
With the ten of diamonds, I am the winner.

Imagine yourself winning the game, and feeling good about your achievement.

Staying in the Flow

Keeping money flowing

It is quite normal for the money in your
life to ebb and flow like the tide, but when
the tide has been out for too long, something
may be wrong. If you're having problems with
money, see if any of the following applies to you.

Are you focusing on what you don't have? If you are focusing
mainly on what is lacking in your life, then you are
encouraging more of the same.

Do you believe that you deserve more money? Without the
belief that you deserve to be wealthy, you are likely to hold
yourself back.

Are you continuously foolish with money? If you continuously abuse the way you handle your finances, then being or staying wealthy could be difficult.

Do you back up your intention with the appropriate action? If you fail to take action on your money inspirations, then cash is unlikely to materialize.

If you're struggling with any of the above, make up a phrase set in the present tense, to help you overcome your weak spot. For example, you could say to yourself, "I now handle my money wisely." Tell yourself this frequently, with feeling, and see how quickly your attitude changes.

Affirmation of prosperity spell

You will need:
magazines or catalogs
scissors
a large piece of paper
glue
pine oil
something to give away

This spell will help you attract the prosperous life you want.

Begin by making yourself a treasure map. Look at magazines or catalogs and cut out pictures that symbolize what you would like to bring into your life. These could include pictures of money, houses, people, or anything that represents a prosperous lifestyle. Stick these pictures onto your piece of paper to make a collage.

During a Full Moon, put your collage in front of you. Anoint the back of each corner with pine oil. Then, looking at your collage, say the following affirmations:

I now create the life I want to live.
I am deserving of prosperity.
I am guided to make the right decisions.
I am open and receptive to all that is good.
I show gratitude.

Imagine yourself living the life you want and having all the
money and possessions you desire. See them coming to
you with ease.

The next day, give away whatever you have chosen to part
with. This could be an item of clothing or object to a thrift shop,
or a donation of some kind as a symbol of your gratitude.

Picture credits

Ann Shore, London-based designer, stylist and owner of Story:

4 Wilkes Street, London E1 6QF

44 (0)20 7377 0313

story@btconnect.com

Personal selection of old and new furniture and accessories. Afternoons only.